The Mother Word
An Exploration
of the Visual

Mattie McClane
Myrtle Hedge Press

The Mother Word: An Exploration of the Visual
Copyright © 2017 by Myrtle Hedge Press
Kernersville NC

The ISBN 978-0-9722466-7-5
The Library of Congress Control Number 201745637

Printed in the United States of America

All rights reserved. No part of this book may be used or reproduced in any manner whatsoever without the written permission by the authors, except in the case of brief quotations embodied in critical articles and reviews. This is a creative work and any resemblance to any real person is coincidental.

To Nancy Huse

Contents

Contents	v
The Chandelier	1
Uncertainty	51
Segolene Royal	53
Bricks	55
At 30 or 50	56
Chance Meeting	62
The Veil	64
Vagabonds	66
My Mother's Voice	69
Winners and Losers	71
Reminders	74
The Willow	76
Treacherous Road	79
Early Tree	82
About the Author	85

The Chandelier

Sunlight warmth
on the skin
on a temple
light flickers
flashes
with rushing speed
and blinds
an eye
in moments
something peaceful
a settling inward
speckled white moisture
forms mountains

in the sky
not threatening
the weather
has passed
leaving its drops
on lawns
on the heads
of people
driving convertibles
the rugged jeep
with a manual
transmission
confounding
a new generation
who reach
for uncertain stories
of allegiance

to the flag
recited in elementary schools
with written-on
dusty chalkboards
the light comes
in through low rectangular
windows
with steel frames
with a view
of parking lots
and paths
to statues
of saints, martyrs
covered
for Good Friday
the bright air prompts
a trip to the river

to a shop
with a broken sidewalk
a door handle
with a place
for a thumb
to press open
to relics
wooden bookcases
with Life magazines
award-winning
photography
for a 60s audience
thick leather volumes
cases of jewelry
with stories
of anniversaries
a loving forgotten couple

displays
of pins worn
on the chests
of matronly aunts
floral designs
semi-precious stones
from estate sales
everything
the dead remember
on special occasions
the antique rosaries
said how
many prayers
on an anxious day
or when one felt
particularly close
to the Lord

the metal crucifix
is tarnished
there are tea cups
a few strays
from china cabinets
in Victorian homes
only blocks away
from an international port
where sailors
came buying gifts
for sweethearts
in the day
of glamour girls
from the store's ceiling
hangs a crystal chandelier
and a string
with a price tag

cut heavy glass
in three tiers
sparkling radiant
a treasure
preservation
of departed souls
the family pictures
with an unusually tall son
in suspenders
women
wearing wool sweaters
and long skirts
entertained suitors
under its light
the patriarch
read newspapers
in armchairs

while the dog
slept in corners
under a table
the illumination
was enough to see
aspects of living
cutting up
a whole chicken
for dinner
before the great wars
when water
was pumped
from the deep well
to the kitchen
and a white stove
with a see-through door
featured hot coal

burning above
the fixture
with its six candles
witnessed brothers
arm wrestling
the heirs
who were the prize
of the group
college bound
while sisters fussed
with yarn
and scissors
measuring material
for everyday dresses
In the morning
the sun's rays
project colors

on the walls
telling stories
when white light
is broken down
refracted
into spectra
they are details
the personalities
of history
culture
exposed
in narratives
poetry
fairy tales
for lazy
onlookers
who go fishing

in coastal waterways
and dine
in restaurants
with pictures
on the wall
of the local catch.

Red Scare

Russians interfered
in the presidential election
the list of aides grows
the people
are not happy
even though
they do not remember
Sacco and Vanzetti
worries about

foreigners
immigrants
or Dorothy Day's
leftist companions
who hid out
in shoddy houses
were subject
to raids
hearings shaking
up Hollywood
the lovers
of the downtrodden
the poor
who worked
in factories
in mechanical yards
taking lunches

in sturdy pails
while soup lines
of unemployed men circled
the busy blocks
of cities with high rises
far from stockyards
where animals
came in trucks
to a four-way stop sign
the hired men
were butchers
meat-cutters
who fed
their children bread
potatoes
boiled bones
into broth.

Every good journalist
wrote exposes
about labor conditions
and wealth
was pervasive
in a different part
of town sweet cream
dark coffees
afternoon evening
beef roasts
and gravy over
the entire plate
soft down pillows
never dreaming
of unfortunate others

Bedtime stories

the bad wolf
dresses as a grandma
the menaces
are hidden
like the thief
who is never caught
red handed
when the myrtles
branches blow
scarlet flowers bloom
too early
in the year
and the temperature climbs
the pavement
red hot
everyone
is skeptical

of Russia
another scare only
this time
those who lack
are ignored
The real threat
the caution sign
the warning
in bold letters
isn't Marxist
or some theory
to soothe
the masses
about a dingy existence
coal miners
want more holes
in the earth

tunnels lined
with underground lights
when the dust
becomes heavy
alarms go off
red is danger
the planet lets
us know
of peril
and we are required
to listen

An ill-considered apple
was glossy red
the forbidden fruit
in the garden
with cherries

rhubarb stalks
so attractive
to the eye.
Watch that color
its spirit its power
in red silk ties
politician's garb
highlighting tan skin
the ability
to bamboozle
to provoke
the bullfighter's taunt.

Cinderella's Orange
When a pumpkin
is transformed
into a carriage

the middle-class
magical hope
is that the young woman
would not suffer
cruelty anymore
a lottery winner
in a garden fruit
with wheels
and footmen
a comfortable ride
to the palace
reveals dreams
wishful thinking
the harsher reality
a downside
with no leniency
when men show

off jumpsuits
at authorities jails
petty theft
armed robbery
and worse
the orange
of imprisonment
of being charged
dissidents
political prisoners
revolutionaries
ardent activists
rebel pens
that tout
uneasy truths
brilliant boat-rockers
locked away

alienated
and lonesome
with public defenders
plea bargains
rushed work
the innocent
are in with the rest
who wait
for court dates

High visibility
the hunter's outfit
a man is no deer
in the field.
the orange
jacket tips off
other's with guns.

detour signs
cannot be denied
like reflector cones
in road construction.
a man guides
his pick-up truck
through obstacles
a buck hanging
out of the tailgate
construction workers
wear bright vests
so others can see them.
life preservers
tying in front
the bulkiness
rough straps
so rescued boaters

can be reached and taken
up from the water

A fiery ball
spreading orange
on the horizon line
at sunset
a glowing star
burning
more heat
world tension
rogue nations
the possibility
of thermo nuclear war
wildfires
from climate change
orange needles

dried forests
Pedrogao Grande
hellish flames
consuming houses
businesses
terrorism
ever-looming
as beach-goers retire
shaking
off sand
with open car doors
putting children
into automobiles
people look
to the West over
water marsh
grasses to see

the searching
ibis's beak

Yellow Gold
A ring signals commitment
between lovers
individuals
who met
on the Internet
they might stand
at the altar
with sacred
adornments
on its surface
a weighty treasure
a would-be
pirate's booty

from rascals
who sailed
the ocean
and took whatever
they wanted locked
crates
chests full
of ornate
drinking cups
crafted goblets
the chalice
coin stacks
depicting the king's
insignia
his official
reign beads
strung

into fashionable necklaces
candle holders
the world
plots
clamors
for gold
at what price?
The prospector
with a pouch
of dust
wants to buy supplies
hammers
and picks
People will be
are betrayed
for riches
profit-mongers

put bounties
on the heads
of the poor
who want
thrift store rolls
the rounded tops
of warm loaves
with butter
sweet spread
instead
of the new military
industrial complex
corporate avarice
the despot's
opulence
the flashy ways
of authoritarian

government
subsidized
oil companies
in budget priorities
where invisible
humanity
is not counted.
Geography
is featured
in yellow magazines
best known
for poignant
pictures
of Arctic melting
of famine
the plight
of indigenous tribes

Green Fields

A long road trip
going home
to the Midwest
past cornfields
soybeans
sweeping green
for miles pines
beside farmhouses
wind buffers
where children
grow, the world
is growing
sprouting
flowering
beautiful grasses
every leaf

in summer
delights
the eye
seeing steeples
the courthouses
the neighborhoods
tended yards
the Paris Agreement
where citizens
care about green
trees cooling
the planet
the breeze blowing
through
covered limbs
the child
reaches an age

when called
an adult
experience
is all
that is needed
to know
about politicians
and how dollars
affect policy
big money cash
that keeps lawmakers
from saving
the shiny river
from chemicals
surrounded
by poplars
and other vegetation

that sucks
the water
into life.
the people
need plants
bushes vines
weeds
the stately oak tree
in front
of landmark houses
that have
been there
for over
a 100 years
on the streets
stray clumps blades
in the cracks

of concrete
cyclists watch
for emerald glass
on the road
the shattered
premium
beer bottle
thrown
from a party
where a blanket
was placed
on the ground
in the park
land set aside
so citizens
can play
musicians tune

instruments
on bandstands
they compete
with the faraway noise
of mowers
people want
more green
summer relaxation
the feeling
on being
with nature
canopied woodlands
hidden life
tiny heartbeats
of squirrels
raccoons
munching deer herds

opossum
the birds
that sit on branches
singing
and flying
through the day

Mother Blue
A seaside gazebo
protection
against the sun
the ocean mirrors
the cloudless sky
showing
little separation
between
air and water

the mother
and the child.
the self
sexual identity
is not yet
formed
the two are one
in rhythm
in motion
the body protrudes
goes into workplaces
into grocery
stores nestles
into a queen-sized bed
the womb
covers all
flowing

like the blue planet
where people live
on seven continents
discovered
by explorers
adventure
sanctuary
seekers
who set off
in uncharted seas
in storms
when crews
were washed overboard
swimmers
for survival
for pleasure
in clubby pools

women athletes enter
roped race lanes
the freestyle
breaststroke
backstroke
butterfly
timed events
all the ways
to reach back
to beginnings
to amniotic fluids
to sustenance
to victory
blue ribbons
to awards
the enjoyment
is the surf

rolling forward
and back
movement
where pelicans
hover over
curled waves
the birds
are hungry
for mullet
small fish
glittery scales
while humans return
to cultural icons
Mother Mary
in an ample
draping gown
with a border

the whale
a mammal
that nurtures
her calf
in blue seas
and migrates
up the Eastern coast

Vineyard Violet
Philosophers
the mystics
the teachers
in book-lined rooms
in studies
in classrooms
at the academy
the imagination

the invention
is full of ideas
with a sketch
or a plan
speculation
about the view
from the top
of purple mountains
the height
the depth
the width
of the soul
in paintings
in essays
in poetry
when the bard
creates rhythms

with language
that comes
in dreams
the apparitions
the characters
who play a part
in night chatter
the half realities
when the mind
interacts
awakes
to its concerns
its desires
sleep patterns
its knowledge
of good
and evil collide

into what
can be discerned
remembering
scenes
absurdities
before consecrated wine
touches
the tongue
uplifting spirits
the Concord grapes
the work
of human hands
celebrating saints
worshiping one
in a mock royal robe
the burdens
the suffering

of this earth
that redeems
bar flies
pancake house patrons
firemen
builders
devout sisters
holy priests
late-shift nurses
at a restaurant
serving breakfast
24 hours a day
to the tired
and weak
the crosses
the passions
of ordinary people

are realized
and sometimes relieved

White Light

Light moves away
from crystals
colors disappear
from the walls.
the sun moves on
shooting beams
behind clouds
the brightest white
the radiance
a gleaming spectacle
a transfiguration
touching
the water forming

a lighted path
as if for a hiker
a rambler
a wanderer
with a walking stick
on flickering waves
like jumping molten silver
it points the way
a widening swath
to the stories
to hesitant tales
evading only
in moments
what constitutes
glorious light
the hues
reunited

recombined
in discovery
the revelations
of the visual
the mother word
in particulars
in wave lengths
specific objects
earth's lifeblood
where secrets
are no longer
kept all people
will know
in darkest corners
in the tightest cell
in miserable slums
the beginning

the middle
and the end
the theme
the verdict
uncovered sight
healed eyes
of justice
of mercy
the last pages
of age old mysteries
shining through

Uncertainty

Wind sends pollen
into the streets
like revolutionary peasants
it commands seagulls
to take an alternate route
over parking lots
They dance, sail
to new sideways
steps in the blue air.
The wind bends trees
so they look haunted
cruel, stooped
and crooked.

The ocean wind
is a force
to be reckoned
with relief
on a hot day
it is not human
but grinds the rocks
my untied hair
moves into knots; it slows
me down. I haven't
decided if it is friendly.

Segolene Royal

The woman wears white
a tailored jacket
for a French candidate
running for president
Who will tell her story
about what the sex
believes after having young?
She promises fairness, one
should be treated like another.

That makes it difficult
to change directions
from old ways

the nurturing habits
reserved for children
A woman brings her whole
self wherever she goes.

She does not escape
history with success
It will not be easy
to find a world
that genuinely cares
with no favorites
but she would be there
in mighty decisions
in front of a microphone
standing on a platform
wrapped in state colors.

Bricks

Sandbur sunlight pricks
the turquoise clouds green,
and workers take bricks hard
and stack them into buildings
There is glory and white mud
on their shoes; they walk up the hill
and are celebrated for making
something that lasts beyond
bookmaker's conversations
and author notes. Their creation
will stand when the cloth hangs
in museums tourists people uncles
pass paying eight dollars to come in.

At 30 or 50

I thought I'd try
to tell stories
about fathers
and mothers
essences
on a daily drive
to where pelicans touch
the wild surf
so confident
and assured
I won't be
like a pelagic bird
that waits

for handfuls
of yellow popcorn
from weekend tourists
who leave
on Sunday.

What have I wanted?
the room with a writing table
the one across
from the river.
I am a child
of tar roads
of redwing blackbirds
once innocent
never taught
who looked
for interesting people

sharing ideas
lighting up
at the sound
of a beloved's name
or the person
who brought
birthday cakes
at 30 or 50
it was all
the same. It was all
the same, charming.
they used
that word
at a candidate's forum,
the perfect moderator
whom I loved.

I loved him, too.
the way
we see ourselves
without checked
paper boxes
fluid identity
where kings
and queens
are on the same table.

It is important
to talk of love now.
There seems
so little extra
a small serving
for everyone
people left hungry

in many ways
tired of neighbors
after years
of watching them
come and go
four hours away
where the green
stays forever
on the coast
with briny red roses
the winter is windy
and the buzzards
are chased off
with a broomstick
they do not impress me
the pelican takes what
is vital from the sea

never getting wet
until its dive
from the middle of the sky.

Chance Meeting

Now you are gone,
and I will never see
you again. How
was it that we came
to share the same
city and time
went to common
department stores
corner gas stations
sat at red lights
to view landmark buildings
while the traffic
passed people

keeping appointments
just to return home.
I can locate you
if I am silent hear
you laughing, drumming
up followers
in old neighborhoods
many hours
near Westminster
through lighted windows
the chase after holiness.

The Veil

I have a sheer veil
forgotten from one
who didn't get cold feet
but made a promise
and went to Tennessee
to the hilly land
near horse farms
high rises, music city
the item is long,
and it is not good
at covering imperfections.
I am not modest
I am not shy

I am rather outspoken
lift the material
almost see-through
the floor's sweep.

Vagabonds

Elderly people leave
too soon. They pack
up their bags
for auctions, sales
stocking hats
for bargain seekers
odorous sweaters
of an entire life
the remote control
in one spot
near the television,
and I miss them
their humble stories

told over again
with the same delight
in long distant calls
when everything
is explained
every family action
is reflected upon
and never missed.
Old people
take flight
and you might think
they are rude
to pick up their things
to go on a jaunt
they swoop through
the air glide
through eternity

play strategic cards
with roommates
They are hard to love
because they are fickle
canceling rain
drenched newspapers
neighbors bring
in the mail. You
never know when
they might skip town
carrying
their stories with them.

My Mother's Voice

I sing with my mother's voice
rich
deep
penetration
that goes beyond
our space
our time
into the past.
It cries
for our lovers
while nurturing
our children
concocting

sweet rhymes
that run
gush
pour
from our enclosures
our wombs
into stillness
into birth
into song

Winners and Losers

A bread heel
was left
after someone
fed the birds
six seagulls
discovered
the slice
on the pavement
of a favorite
tourist overlook
fluttering chaos
came next
each gull took

a turn holding
the prize
in its beak
until another
would fly in
and steal it
from its temporary owner
the exchange
went on for
a few minutes
until finally
a victor
flew away
with the piece
seemingly safe
over the water
but the cumbersome square

was too heavy
and dropped
into the sea.
only the lucky fish
didn't go without

Reminders

You will need
to provide us
with an email address
so we can send you
thoughtful reminders
our coupons
latest rewards
from sales meetings
from the people
who wear
company shirts
and call midday
about laminations

a completed order
team energy
a restless wind
the dogwood
petals fall
on the sidewalk
up to the steps
to the front
door nature
does not keep them
in the spam folder.

The Willow

I believe
in wind dances
and leaves
the way the sun
shines into
your eyes
and all is silver
and stretching out.

Then I remember
how hard
it is to love what
is explained

in books or not
explained in books.
How difficult
it is to stand
there letting trees
pass as drawings
pencil or ink
illustrations
rather than live
furrowed trunks.

I'm not complaining
but my thin rings
are numbered
in years and too many
times I've bent
to the ground

waiting for
the weather
to stop
so I could rise
and shake myself
straight
back stunned
and aching
and wondering why
the willow
sways sweeps
never falling
onto waiting grass.

Treacherous Road

The morning brings
a rare snowfall
the streets
salted for Southern
drivers who fire
up their engines
with imaginings
of a green flag
slick programs
with driver biographies
full beer coolers
the anticipation
deafening noise

the loud rumble
of the big race
and in some houses
the weatherman says
stores are closed
schools are empty
on account of ice
on sidewalks.
I will stay home
like the rest
and write opinions
for newspapers
in a furniture town
with two main drags
past churches
corporate headquarters
they have all

heard by now
that it is not safe.

Early Tree

A color wheel turns
in front
of a spotlight
onto silver
branches tinting
and reflecting a hue
in a crooked
little house
near an abandoned
rail station
never to become
a restaurant
it is a good thing

to remember
spirit pieces
and old friends
when the cedar seed
is broken
open memories
are pinched
living green
under curious nails
in a Midwestern town
where I visit
where I imagine
elderly furnace heat
and feel Christmas peace.

About the Author

Mattie McClane (Kristine A. Kaiser) is an American novelist, poet, and journalist. She is the second and youngest daughter born to James L. and Shirlie I. Myers in Moline, Illinois. Her father was a commercial artist and her mother worked as a secretary.

McClane's parents divorced when she was eight years old. Her mother remarried attorney John G. Ames and the new couple moved to a house beside the Rock River. The river centrally figures in McClane's creative imagination. She describes her childhood as being "extraordinarily free and close to nature."

McClane moved to Colorado and married John Kaiser in 1979 in Aurora, just East of Denver.

They then moved to Bettendorf, Iowa, where they had three children. John worked as a chemist. Mattie became interested in politics, joining the local League of Women Voters. According to McClane, she spent her 20s "caring for young children and working for good government."

She graduated from Augustana College with a B.A. degree in the Humanities. She began writing a political column for Quad-Cities Online and Small Newspaper Group, based in Illinois.

Her family moved to Louisville, Kentucky where she continued with her journalism and then earned an M.A. in English from the University of Louisville. Critically acclaimed author Sena Jeter Naslund directed her first creative thesis, "Unbuttoning Light and Other Stories," which was later published in a collection.

She was accepted to the University of North Carolina at Wilmington's M.F.A. in Creative Writing Program, where she wrote the short novel *Night Ship*, working under the tutelage of Pulitzer Prize winning author Alison Lurie. McClane studied with Dennis Sampson in poetry also. She graduated in 1999.

She would write a column for the *High Point Enterprise* in North Carolina. She would later write for the *News and Observer*. McClane has regularly published commentary for over 25 years.

Mattie McClane is the author of *Night Ship: A Voyage of Discovery* (2003), *River Hymn: Essays Evangelical and Political* (2004), *Wen Wilson* (2009), *Unbuttoning Light: The Collected Short Stories of Mattie McClane* (2012), *Now Time* (2013), and *Stations of the Cross* (2016).

She lives in North Carolina.

www.ingramcontent.com/pod-product-compliance
Lightning Source LLC
Chambersburg PA
CBHW050604300426
44112CB00013B/2064